Introduction

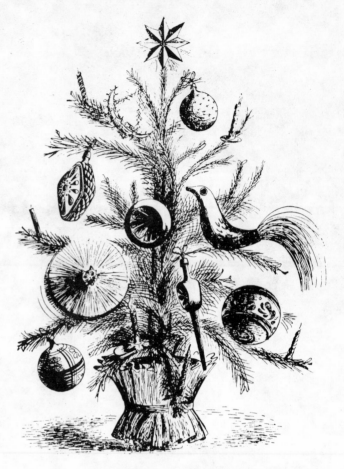

From the spectacular point of view, especially as regards outdoor illumination and decorations, the United States leads the world in Christmas showmanship. In the realm of commercial activity, no other nation anticipates Christmas for so long a period with so much sharply focused advertising. The excitement and the rustle and bustle that attend Christmas on every level of American life outdistance that of practically every country in the world. This is said not in a boasting manner, but rather to illustrate the way in which Christmas in our country has evolved since the close of the Civil War. Uncounted millions of Christmas cards, yards of ribbon and wrappings, and all the trappings of the holiday season are mass-produced to such an extent that Christmas is becoming perhaps too much standardized.

On the other hand, nowhere else in the world within the boundaries of a single nation is Christmas observed with a greater variety of customs and traditions. Every country and practically every region of the globe have descendants here. Within the past two decades, removed by only one or two generations from life in Europe, many of our citizens have shown a growing awareness of their cultural heritage. In their desire to preserve it, they are rediscovering and reviving old folkways, modes, and manners of doing things that have given tradition itself a new kind of significance. Their enthusiasm is imbued with great reverence, a sense of devotion, and a love for the ways of the past.

However, this is not to say that contemporary happenings and new ways of observing and enjoying Christmas are being ignored. Santa Claus, the Christmas tree, poinsettias, Christmas cards, carols, the immortal message of Dickens, and a host of other holiday diversions—all contribute to making our Christmas a time of great exuberance and joy. Throughout all the states—in public displays, in churches, in private homes—manger scenes are enjoying an unprecedented wave of popularity. Despite the glamour of the community Christmas tree, amid the gleam of electric lights and all the outdoor pageantry, Christmas in millions of American homes across the land is essentially a feast of the heart and the hearth as elsewhere in the world. Within the confines of the family circle, it glows and shines as it was intended that the birthday of the Christ Child should be celebrated. Grandma's recipes for cookies and cakes are cherished and often shared. The sentiment linked with

Let's Celebrate Christmas

The American Christmas: Its Customs and Pageantry

An *ideals* Publication

IDEALS PUBLISHING CORP., MILWAUKEE, WIS. 53201
© COPYRIGHT MCMLXXVII, PRINTED AND BOUND IN U.S.A.
ISBN 0-89542-289-1 295

CONTENTS

compiled and designed by

Mark Clifford Brunner

Managing Editor, Ralph Luedtke

Photographic Editor, Gerald Koser

Production Editor, Stuart L. Zyduck

White House Photo

Right: The Macy's Parade in New York on Thanksgiving Day officially marks the opening of the long holiday season across the country. Bottom right: With ruddy cheeks and his snow-white beard blowing in the wind, Father Christmas pulls into Edaville, Massachusetts, "under his own steam" but just ahead of the Edaville Railroad's Christmas Festival Special. Bottom left: In Williamsburg, Virginia, the Christmas season is ushered in by the Grand Illumination of the city. The Historic Area glows from the cressets of blazing pinewood and the "white lighting" candlelight in the windows of shops, homes and public buildings.

5

Courtesy, The Seattle Historical Society

Each Christmas season American community Christmas celebrations, though separated by miles, climates and cultures, are tied together by the brilliance of color. Top: A colorfully garbed Russian Orchestra performs at the 1974 Seattle "Christmas Around the World" festival. Left: The sparkle of thousands of shining lights decorate the Plaza in Kansas City, Missouri.

Courtesy, The Missouri Division of Tourism

Right: Christmas in Hollywood: rows of trees, fashioned around the lampposts, stars and bells strung across the famous boulevard in the movie capital of the world set the stage for gift shopping in Hollywood. Bottom: The world's largest living Christmas Tree stands in Wilmington, North Carolina. This three-hundred-year-old live oak is lighted with 4,000 multi-colored bulbs and is viewed each December by a quarter of a million persons. Its limb-spread is 110 feet and its height, 55 feet. The General Grant tree near Singer, California, is certainly the tallest representative Christmas tree in the world; due to its immense size, however, it has never been decorated.

Color by Josef Muench

Courtesy, The Greater Wilmington Chamber of Commerce

7

Top: In Lumpkin, Georgia, visitors watch as the log lighter performs the Burning of the Yule Log ceremony. Three times, he sprinkles the log with oil and expresses a traditional wish each time. He then lights the wood with a piece of the previous year's log. The small wooden cross he holds was saved from the log and will be used to light next years' log. Left: "Christmas Tree Lane" in Altadena, California. The lane is comprised of about 150 deodar cedar trees, all about 80 feet tall. Every year the trees are decorated with nearly 10,000 lights which illuminate the avenue its entire one-mile length.

Guy Burgess

A Colorado family celebrates a traditional Bavarian Christmas.

ornaments treasured from year to year is akin to that shared by people the world over. Churches and Sunday schools make the true meaning ring as they compete with the activities of the mercantile world. Nevertheless, the same excesses and distortions that plagued our forefathers are still with us.

In Boston, New York, Philadelphia, Cleveland, Dallas, and Baton Rouge—from San Diego to Seattle, from Denver to Atlanta—everywhere that one turns, the distinct flavor of Christmas as formerly enjoyed somewhere in the Old World is emulated and loved. However, it is in city neighborhoods, in suburban communities, and in small towns that the spirit of Christmas is felt most intimately. Wherever people are closely linked by common interests, the feast of Christmas burns with an especially bright glow and rings with a fidelity of tone that is easy to sense. Christmas Eve on Boston's Beacon Hill, with its bell ringers and carol singers, its softly lighted windows and garlanded doorways, is vivid enough to make one feel that Charles Dickens himself might be giving a reading of the *Christmas Carol* in some nearby auditorium as he did a century ago.

A visit to Duke of Gloucester Street in Williamsburg at Christmas carries one back to eighteenth-century Virginia since the flavor of an old English Christmas has there been preserved in all its colorful detail. In this same community, the lighting of the Christmas tree, inaugurated in 1843, brings back memories of a nineteenth-century Christmas. Pennsylvania offers the Moravian observances at Bethlehem and Lititz, the Mummers' Parade on New Year's Day in Philadelphia, and the Christmas yards or *putzes* of the Pennsylvania Dutch.

The Christmas tree, introduced to America by the German settlers of the commonwealth of Pennsylvania in the eighteenth century, has become our national symbol of Christmas. Perhaps our country's most distinct contribution to the Christmas traditions of the world is the community Christmas tree found in nearly every city and town, large and small, all across the country, and in the elaborate lighting effects on buildings, trees, and shrubbery seen everywhere. Little else that we enjoy at Christmas can be called truly American in origin, since our Christmas heritage is a composite of that of the whole world.

Daniel J. Foley

From CHRISTMAS THE WORLD OVER by Daniel J. Foley, Copyright 1963 by the author. Reprinted with the permission of the publisher, CHILTON BOOK COMPANY, Radnor, Pennsylvania.

The Origin of Christmas Customs

We take most of our Yuletide customs for granted, but most of them are very old and have been passed from country to country . . . generation to generation. A great many of them stem from a true religious beginning, even though it may be different from what we, today, think of as religion.

Mistletoe

The word mistletoe is derived from the Saxon *mistl-tan*, meaning "a different twig," and there's an interesting legend about this pearl-berried green. It seems that Balder, a Scandinavian hero, was killed by an arrow made from a mistletoe tree branch. The gods were angered by this and decreed that from that time on mistletoe should be nothing but a parasite . . . and should cause no more trouble. The berries, according to Norse mythology, were the tears of the goddess Frigga and were shed at the death of her son "Balder the Beautiful." It is from this legend that kissing beneath the mistletoe came about; the kiss is a symbol of peace and an assurance that mistletoe can still cause no sorrow, but will foster affection instead. Our custom of hanging a sprig of mistletoe in doorways, to invoke romance, is said to be an adaption of the Druids' custom of placing it above the fireplace to please the sylvan spirits.

Another legend which is perhaps more closely related to the real meaning of Christmas is that the Cross was made of mistletoe branches which until that time had been a noble tree. Because of the cruel use to which it was put, the growth was then condemned to live as a parasite on others.

Holly

This red-berried, glossy-leaved shrub is prevalent in our decorations at Christmastime. Its use is traced to the early Romans who sent holly boughs to their friends during the feast of Saturnalia which occurred at about the time our Yuletide does. The early Christians continued this custom of using holly as gifts, but fashioned it into wreaths to symbolize the crown of thorns . . . the red berries symbolic of drops of blood. From that time on, the holly wreath has stood for timelessness, its endless circle being the emblem of eternity. Originally, Holly was called *Holy*; yellowed church records read: "Item for holy and ivye at Christmas . . . Due for holy decoration" . . . and so on.

Poinsettia

The velvety, scarlet poinsettia plant originally came from the hills of our neighbor, Mexico, although in some unknown way it migrated to Europe. Perhaps Cortez's army took plants or seeds back and presented them to the court of Spain whence the flower spread throughout Europe; no one is sure. It was introduced into our country by Dr. Joel Roberts Poinsett, an American envoy to Mexico in the 1930s, who was a great nature lover and spent much time roaming the Mexican hills where he was en-

Holly decorates the flaming plum pudding.

tranced by what the Mexicans called fire-flower which grew in great profusion. The flaming blooms were so unlike any American flowers that Dr. Poinsett brought back a few to the United States. Assisted by a friend who was a florist, he experimented in raising them. It took several years to perfect the blooms; but because American florists recognized their beauty, they persisted until they succeeded. Today the poinsettia—named for their finder—is one of our most popular Christmas flowers, even though it has no religious significance.

Bayberry Candles

Candles made from bayberries were first made in Puritan homes and have long been burned at Yuletide. The sturdy Puritans gathered the gray bayberries from the shrubs which grew on the salt marshes near the sea. They then obtained the wax from them to make the candles, or dips, as they called them. The fragrance from a bayberry candle is distinctive and can only be found in the wax from real bayberry shrubs; imitations are in appearance only. They have been called "good luck candles," based upon an old belief that they bring good luck and good fortune to any home in which they burn at Christmastime. From this legend comes the saying: "A bayberry candle burned to its socket . . . brings luck to the home and wealth to the pocket." Like the burning of conventional candles, a bayberry one in the window on Christmas Eve is meant as a welcome to a lonely stranger. This is an outgrowth of the Star lighting the way for the shepherds to find the manger on that first Christmas.

Christmas Greens

Greenery is used extensively in our homes at holiday time to give a festive look. This is no modern idea. The early pagans cut branches from evergreen

CUTTING CHRISTMAS TREES

trees, carried them to their temples, and worshiped them for maintaining life throughout the long winter. In King Solomon's time, greens were used in all the sacred rites of the religious festivals. Since the days of Druids, greens of one kind or another have hung over lintel and hearth.

Christmas Carols

Carols have been sung for ages and have come down to us as a rich heritage, the singing of them at Yuletide is one of the happy highlights of the season. The word carol is derived from *cantare*, which means to sing, and *rola*, meaning to interject, as for joy. According to tradition, the first Christmas carol was sung on the very first Christmas... "Fear not... Glory to God in the highest and on earth peace, goodwill toward men."

For ever since that immortal night on the plains of Bethlehem when the star guided shepherds and Wise Men to the manger, songs have been sung to honor Christ's birthday. According to legendary history, the first true Christmas carol was not written or sung until the thirteenth century, when St. Francis of Assisi composed songs for a part of a sacred service about the Nativity and to accompany a tableau representing the manger scene. At first these early carols were sung only in churches; but their beauty and meaning made them so well loved that they gradually became universal. Now after nearly two thousand years, the Christmas carol is still one of the strongest expressions of the real Christmas spirit.

Greeting Cards

Christmas cards are sent to friends at holiday time and are the newest of the Christmas customs. The first one appeared in 1846 when an English artist, Joseph Cundall, made some decorated cards for a very busy man to send to his

"Preparing Christmas Greens," by T. De Thulstrup
From Harper's Weekly, Dec. 25, 1880.

Another interesting custom is the minting of Christmas stamps. This has been an American tradition since 1962 and has been adopted by other countries in recent years.

A reproduction of the first known Christmas Card, created for Sir Henry Cole by John C. Horsley in 1843.

friends; this saved the friend writing many letters. The idea was new, the recipients became interested, and the next year others copied the idea. In 1862 a lithographer, who felt that it was a mighty good way to express greetings, issued several differently designed cards, all carrying "Merry Christmas" incorporated in the designs. From then on sending Christmas cards spread like wildfire until today we have no idea what forms and styles these cards may be. Some are lovely and carry a real spiritual meaning, others are comical.

Christmas Gifts

It's a pleasure to give presents at Yuletide since it is truly "more blessed to give than receive." The first gifts were, of course, those given the Holy Babe, although the Roman fathers used to give their sons pieces of gold, torches, and laurel wreaths, hoping these would instill getting wealth, learning, and power into their offsprings' minds. Slaves, too, gave each other colored beads as tokens of affection; but it was not until the first Christmas that gifts as real tokens of love and a part of the true Christmas spirit as we know it, were given.

A group of youngsters delight in a ride on the traditional Yule Log at Colonial Williamsburg, Virginia.

Yule Log

For centuries the Yule log has been a guarantee of warmth, light and safety and was first used by barbarians. They believed that the massive trunks from which the logs were made kept them safe during the winter in their enemy and wolf-infested woods. In fifteenth-century Scandinavia, the Yule log celebration was a picturesque one. A huge log was dragged from the woods to the center of the large manor hall; and then with great pomp the fire was started with a piece of charred wood kept from the Yule log of the previous year. This brand had been carefully stored because it was supposed to provide security against fire and to ward off evil spirits during the year. The freshly lighted Yule log, which burned for days, was symbolic of promise and disruptive of all ill feeling.

In medieval England, the Yule log was a huge one selected weeks before Christmas. On Christmas Eve it was wound with greens, dragged to the great hall at the head of a procession of singing merry-

Hanging Christmas stockings in anticipation of Santa Claus's arrival on Christmas Eve has long been a tradition in Vermont.

makers, and there greeted with happy cheers. To them the Yule log was a definite symbol of good cheer. One by one, the jolly folks would sit upon the garlanded log, sing or hum a snatch of a Christmas carol, then salute the log with a casual kiss—an assurance of good luck until the next Yuletide.

The huge log was then dragged to the hearth while the group crowded about and eagerly watched the log being "touched off" with the *brand* from the preceeding year's log. If the fire went out, it was a sign of bad luck, but this

very rarely happened. But since it *could* happen, the faces around the log—lighted only by it since the rest of the hall was dark—bore anxious expressions until a steady fire was assured. This Yule log ceremony is still carried on in some parts of England.

Hanging Stockings

Children like to hang their stockings up on Christmas Eve. This tradition springs from ancient Holland, where youngsters thought that St. Nicholas made his rounds on a horse named

Slipper. The Amsterdam youngsters set wooden shoes in the chimney corners so that when old "St. Nick" passed he could leave a gift or two in them. The custom spread to France, only the French children put their shoes on the hearth. Eventually instead of shoes, stockings were used and hung by the hearthside.

Christmas Dinner

Christmas dinner is the highlight of the festive days. In Old England the custom of "bringing in the boar's head" was a very important ceremony. Trumpets blared at a stated time; and a procession entered the banquet hall parading the length of the long banquet table at which the diners sat. The boar's head was carried at the head of the procession, on a silver platter. Behind its carriers were pages carrying mustard, which was considered a necessity to aid digestion. Last of all came the plum pudding, a much larger one than those we serve today. From this festivity, our Christmas dinner was evolved, with more modern foods, such as homegrown turkeys, but with the same friendly goodwill centering about the meal.

Mince Pies

Mince pies are associated with the Christmas dinner, and since medieval times have been symbolic of the spices and other gifts brought to the Christ Child by the Wise Men. As early as 1596, these pies were mentioned in books and other printed matter. They were originally called *shrid* pies, then *shredded* pies, and finally *mince* pies. Today they are a traditional dessert for Christmas dinner.

And so we moderns enjoy the Christmas season, carry out many of the old traditions and customs which our forefathers did. We are often unaware of the origins of many that are centuries old and whose beginnings can often give us pause for thought.

Louise Price Bell

Red Kettle on the Corner

The Salvation Army Captain in San Francisco had resolved, in the December of 1891, to provide a free Christmas dinner to 1,000 poor persons. But how would he pay for the food?

As he went about his daily tasks, the question stayed in his mind. Suddenly, his thoughts went back to his days as a sailor in Liverpool, England. On the Stage Landing he saw a large pot, called "Simpson's pot" into which charitable donations were thrown by passersby.

The next morning, he secured permission from the authorities to place a similiar pot at the Oakland ferry landing, at the foot of Market Street. No time was lost in securing the pot and placing it in a conspicuous position, so that it could be seen by all those going to and from the ferry boats. In addition, a brass urn was placed on a stand in the waiting room for the same purpose.

Thus, Captain Joseph McFee launched a tradition that has spread not only

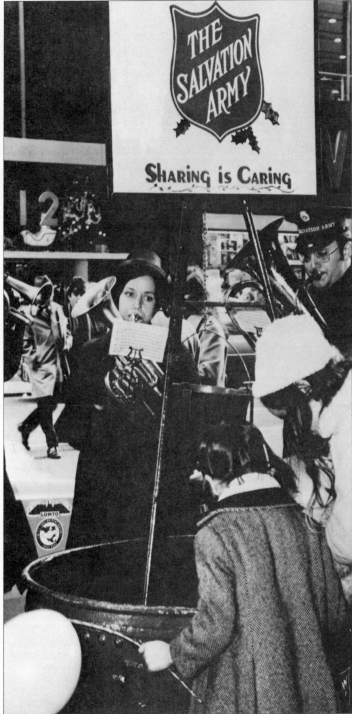

Courtesy. The Salvation Army

activities amd mentioned the contributions to street corner kettles. Shortly afterward, two young Salvation Army officers who had been instrumental in the original use of the kettle, William A. McIntyre and N. J. Lewis, were transferred to the East. They took with them the idea of the Christmas kettle.

In 1897, McIntyre prepared his Christmas plans for Boston around the kettle, but his fellow officers refused to cooperate for fear of "making spectacles of themselves." So McIntyre, his wife and his sister set up three kettles at the Washington Street thoroughfare in the heart of the city. That year, the kettles provided Christmas dinners for 150,000 of Boston's needy.

In 1898, the *New York World* hailed The Salvation Army kettles as "the newest and most novel device for collecting money." The newspaper also observed, "There is a man in charge to see that contributions are not stolen."

In 1901, kettle contributions in New York City provided funds for the first mammoth sit-down dinner in Madison Square Garden, a custom that continued for many years. Today, however, families are given grocery checks so that they can buy and prepare their own dinners at home. The homeless poor are still invited to share holiday dinners and festivities at hundreds of Salvation Army centers.

Kettles are now used in such distant lands as Korea, Japan and Chile, and in many European countries. Everywhere, public contributions to the kettles enable The Salvation Army to bring the spirit of Christmas to those who would otherwise be forgotten—to the aged and lonely, the ill, the inmates of jails and other institutions, the poor and the unfortunate.

In the United States, The Salvation Army annually aids more than 2,000,000 persons at Thanksgiving and Christmas.

throughout the United States, but throughout the world.

By Christmas 1895 the kettle was used in thirty Salvation Army Corps in various sections of the West Coast area. *The Sacramento Bee* of that year carried a description of the Army's Christmas

Kettles have changed since the first utilitarian cauldron set up in San Francisco. Some of the new kettles have such devices as a self-ringing bell and a booth complete with public address system over which the traditional Christmas carols are broadcast. Behind it all though, is the same Salvation Army message, "Share With Others."

A Seal of Christmas Love

The story of the Christmas Seal in America began shortly before the turn of the century when a young doctor was told he had tuberculosis. For centuries this dread disease—known as consumption or the White Plague—meant almost certain death. Dr. Edward Livingston Trudeau decided to spend his remaining years in quiet and peace in a simple cottage at Lake Saranac in his beloved Adirondack Mountains. He expected to die there.

Instead, he began to feel better. Soon it was apparent that his condition was gradually improving. Was rest a major factor, he wondered? Even before he was fully recovered, Dr. Trudeau began to study the relationship between his symptoms and rest. He converted his mountain cottage into a two-patient hospital. When it became apparent that rest helped others recover, funds were raised to add other buildings and facilities.

The news spread. Other physicians opened small tuberculosis sanitariums and there were more miraculous recoveries. In 1904 these physicians, their friends and patients formed what is now known as the American Lung Association, the first voluntary health organization established to fight a specific disease. The first president was, appropriately, Dr. Trudeau. The emblem

Top: A group of Danish Christmas Seals. Note the 1904 seal in the upper left-hand corner. This was the first officially issued Christmas Seal. Right: Germany is just one of many countries which has made use of Christmas Seals for many years.

U.S. Christmas Seals, 1907-1942

chosen was that of early Crusaders—the red double-barred cross.

That same year, a postal clerk named Einar Holboell had an inspiration. Some children dear to him were stricken with tuberculosis. News of the rest treatments in America encouraged him to persuade Danish hospitals to try the same approach. But that would take money. If treatment was to come in time to help his loved ones, funds had to be raised fast!

His own daily work with mail and stamps suggested an idea. Holboell thought of a special kind of penny stamp that would call attention to tuberculosis —a stamp made available during the season of goodwill to others—*Christmas!* His postmaster supported the idea and suggested it to postal authorities. The proposal eventually reached King Christian, who gave it his personal support. Danish citizens responded enthusiastically. The Swedish and Icelandic peoples learned of their neighbor's plan and be-

gan the same program in their own countries. A worldwide crusade was set in motion.

All this happened in 1904 . . . the birth of a great voluntary health organization, the Danish stamp idea, its adoption in Sweden . . . *and one thing more:* A package bearing the Danish Christmas Stamp was delivered to an influential and well-respected Danish-American writer, Jacob Riis. His eye fell on the special stamp with interest. Tuberculosis had killed six of his brothers. Jacob Riis wrote an article pleading that the Christmas Stamp idea be imported to America by some strong organization which could insure its success.

The scene now moves to Delaware where a group of doctors, following Dr. Trudeau's example, had set up a small cottage-hospital on the banks of the Brandywine River. There never seemed to be quite enough money—and in 1907, for lack of just $300 in funds, closing

U.S. Christmas Seals, 1943-1971

seemed inevitable unless a miracle happened. And something of a miracle did occur. One of the doctors, Joseph Wales, appealed to his cousin, Miss Emily Bissell in Wilmington, who was active in the Red Cross and had experience in fund raising. And—she received his letter shortly after reading a reprinting of Jacob Riis's article! What if the same penny-stamp idea could work right here in this country? Miss Bissell went into action! She took the idea to her associates at the Red Cross and they agreed to let her use the Red Cross symbol on the stamp. She then asked the local postmaster if he would help in selling them. Since the Christmas Stamp was not a government issue, the post office could not promote it. Privately, postal officials doubted that selling penny stamps could raise $300. But they agreed to let the energetic young woman put up a stand in the post office lobby to sell her Christmas stamps.

Miss Bissell designed the little stamp herself—a holly wreath with the words Merry Christmas printed in red. Friends helped her get 50,000 of the little stamps printed—along with 2,000 small envelopes to hold 25 stamps each—the envelopes displaying this message:

25 Christmas Stamps, one penny apiece, issued by the Delaware Red Cross to stamp out the White Plague.

Put this stamp with message bright
On every Christmas letter;
Help the tuberculosis fight,
And make the New Year better.

These stamps do not carry any kind of mail but any kind of mail will carry them.

Everyone stopped to look. But for the first three days, sales totaled less than $25 a day. The volunteer workers in the post office lobby began to lose hope. But not Miss Bissell. She reasoned that too few people knew about the Christmas Stamps, and she decided to do something about it. So she traveled to Philadelphia to ask help from a leading newspaper.

The editor she saw was polite but unimpressed. When he said that the paper could not help, Miss Bissell carried the story to her favorite staff writer, Leigh Mitchell Hodges. Hodges examined the stamps, thought for a few minutes, then ran to the office of the editor-in-chief. Quickly outlining Miss Bissell's plan, he exclaimed, "How's this for a slogan: STAMP OUT TUBERCULOSIS!" As a result of Hodges's enthusiasm, the editor offered the entire resources of the paper for the campaign. For the next three weeks, the Christmas Stamps appeared on every page. Then 250,000 more stamps were printed. President Theodore Roosevelt and many members of his cabinet lent their support; and leaders of religious organizations and powerful social groups added their support also. But Miss Bissell and her friends knew they had succeeded when a ragged little newsboy stepped up to the stand in the lobby of the newspaper office, laid down a penny, and said, "Gimme one, m'sister's got it."

More than $3000 was raised in that first Christmas Seal appeal. The little hospital on the Brandywine was saved. The national headquarters of the American Red Cross agreed to sponsor a Christmas Seal campaign the next year —and the next. Each was a bigger success than the year before.

Considering their common concern about tuberculosis, it's not surprising that the two groups, the volunteer health agency headed by Dr. Trudeau and that of Miss Bissell's seals, were soon united, urging people to use the *Christmas Seals* and spreading the word about the new rest treatment for tuberculosis. Volunteers from both groups helped organize educational programs and hospitals for tuberculosis victims throughout the United States. In 1910, the Red Cross and the new voluntary organization jointly issued a *Christmas Seal*. The partnership continued until 1920 when the new organization took over. That year for the first time, the red double-barred cross appeared on the Christmas Seals.

Sweden has also been issuing Christmas seals since 1904.

THE SANTA CLAUS TRADITION

Santa Claus is so much a part of North American childhood that young folk consider him a family friend who lives at the North Pole and makes an annual visit to boys and girls everywhere with the aid of his countless helpers, all dressed alike, who appear in department stores, schools, and even Sunday schools. It is well known that he came to America with the Dutch who settled New York in the seventeenth century; at this time he was called St. Nicholas. Actually, his popularity in the United States stems from "A Visit from St. Nicholas," written in 1822 for the amusement of his own children by a New York clergyman, Dr. Clement C. Moore. The account as presented in the author's *Toys Through the Ages* brings to mind the highlights of the story:

"In 1809, Washington Irving had told the story of St. Nicholas in his *Knickerbocker History*, for the delight of readers in England and America. Some time later, in 1821, a small juvenile was published in New York called *The Children's Friend*. It was a simple book, with eight sparkling color plates and an equal number of verses about 'Santeclaus,' who was shown riding in a sleigh drawn by a single reindeer. This is believed to be the first mention of Santa's reindeer and sleigh, as we know them today.

"Undoubtedly, Dr. Moore had read Irving's book, for it became popular at a time when there were few American writers, and he may have been familiar with *The Children's Friend*. At any rate, he wrote 'A Visit from St. Nicholas,' one of the best-loved and most widely quoted poems ever produced in America. Yet, at the time, he thought it of little merit. To a scholar of Hebrew who was working on a dictionary in that language, a man who was also a distinguished Episcopal preacher and the son of the Bishop of New York, it probably seemed like doggerel. It was simply a bit of verse to delight his own children, and the story was based on his own family and their surroundings.

"Clement Moore's St. Nicholas was no austere saint, such as was portrayed in the Old World Dutch tradition by Washington Irving. Rather, he was a jolly fat

Santa and his elves by George Hinke

man, typical of the prosperous Dutch burghers who had settled New York nearly two centuries earlier. In fact, this inimitable characterization may well have been inspired by a real person, whose name was Jan Duyckinck. He was the caretaker at the Moore home in New York, and it is claimed that he was 'fat, jolly, and bewhiskered' and that he smoked 'a stump of a pipe.' Dr. Moore's St. Nicholas had eight reindeer, each with a name, to enable him to get around in his wonderful sleigh.

"'The Night Before Christmas,' as the poem is fondly referred to, would surely have been forgotten or lost, had it not been for Miss Harriet Butler, the daughter of a clergyman from Troy, New York, who was visiting the Moores that Christmas and heard the clergyman read his poem. She got permission to copy it in her album; and the following year, it appeared anonymously in *The Troy Sentinel* just before Christmas. However, it was not until 1837, when it appeared with a collection of local poetry in book form, that Dr. Moore acknowledged that he was the author. Curiously enough, that same year Robert W. Weir, professor of art at West Point, painted a portrait of Santa Claus, fat and jolly, about to go up a chimney after filling the

Merry Christmas, 1879 lithograph by Thomas Nast.

"Childhood's Faith in Santa Claus—The Christmas Letter."
From Frank Leslie's Illustrated Newspaper, 1887.

stockings he found there.

"The story of Santa's phenomenal rise to fame in the years that followed and his versatility in meeting the requests of children all over the world have been told in scores of books. However, there is more to the story of this wonderful poem. During the latter years of his life, Dr. Moore lived in a large, rambling farmhouse in Newport, Rhode Island. Each year at Christmas since 1954, James Van Alen, a native of this historic community, has presented a dramatic reading of 'A Visit from St. Nicholas,' assisted by his wife and four children from the neighborhood. Dressed in costumes of the period, the group assembles in front of the fireplace of the Newport house for the reading of the poem. Then it is re-enacted in the yard, under floodlights, for the pleasure of the neighbors, followed by carol singing. Later, gifts from the sleigh, which arrives on a float, are distributed to a local children's home. Jimmy Van Alen, as he is popularly known, has organized the House of Santa Claus Society, and hopes to be able to raise enough funds to make the Moore house a historic shrine and Christmas Museum. This enthusiastic champion of Dr. Moore believes that no American has provided more joy for young and old. Mr. Van Alen has written a sequel of seventeen couplets to the poem, because as a child, he thought the poem ended too soon, and he wanted 'to make the fun last longer.' In an interview with Charles D. Rice, he added, 'I used to worry about Father, standing there by the open window as the poem closes. I was afraid he might catch cold, so now I've tucked him safely into bed. I hope Dr. Moore isn't cross at me.' "

Daniel J. Foley

From CHRISTMAS THE WORLD OVER by Daniel J. Foley, Copyright 1963 by the author. Reprinted with the permission of the publisher, CHILTON BOOK COMPANY, Radnor, Pennsylvania.

The All-American Tree

The first Christmas trees we know of in America were those decorated for the children in the German Moravian church's communal settlement in Bethlehem, Pennsylvania, on Christmas Day in 1747. These were not real evergreens, but the European style of wooden pyramids covered with evergreen boughs. A diary tells us that "for this occasion several small pyramids and one large pyramid of green brushwood had been prepared, all decorated with candles and the large one with apples and pretty verses."

Before the 1850s, references to Christmas trees in America were extremely spotty. The second oldest record occurs almost three-quarters of a century after the first, in the form of two sketchbook drawings by John Lewis Krimmel, a Philadelphia artist who made them in 1819 or 1820.

The oldest record we have of Christmas trees in a major American city was in 1825, when Philadelphia's *Saturday Evening Post* described "trees visible through the windows, whose green boughs are laden with fruit, richer than the golden apples of Hesperides, or the sparkling diamonds that clustered on the branches in the wonderful cave of Aladdin."

In 1833 Constantin Hering, a young doctor from Leipzig, arrived in Philadelphia. During his first December in America, homesickness and the memories of his boyhood led him to cross the Delaware River with a friend to cut Christmas trees. Back in Philadelphia with trees on their shoulders, they were followed by a band of curious children. Each year for the next half century, Dr. Hering's marvelous creation was displayed publicly on certain evenings for his friends and for his patients and their friends who wanted to see a German Christmas tree.

On that same Christmas of 1833 Gustave Koerner, a German settler, was living in St. Clair County, Illinois. Since that countryside on the banks of the Mississippi was without evergreens, Koerner and his friends erected their own makeshift Christmas tree. They decorated a sassafras tree with candles, apples, sweets, ribbons, bright paper, hazelnuts and hickory nuts, and polished red haws, the fruit of the hawthorn tree.

As German settlers continued to push into the American West, they took their Christmas custom with them. In 1846 a traveler's letter told of a Christmas tree decorated by German farmers homesteading in Texas. There is no record of when the first evergreen was decorated on the West Coast, but in 1862 a naturalist, William Brewer, visited San Francisco and wrote that he found "Christmas trees are the custom."

Not every German family in America had a Christmas tree, particularly during the first half of the nineteenth century. The custom was still spreading in Germany at that time, and it would not become universal, even there, until the end of the century. Nevertheless, German immigrants were responsible for bringing the Christmas tree to America.

In the mid-nineteenth century Dutch families in New York adopted candlelit

"The Christmas Tree" by F. A. Chapman.

trees, but they decorated them for the New Year rather than Christmas. Santa Claus also arrived a week late, carrying New Year's rather than Christmas presents.

The first Christmas tree to appear in an American church caused a real furor. In 1851 the Reverend Henry Schwan, a thirty-two-year old German immigrant who had arrived in America less than a year before, placed a Christmas tree in his church in Cleveland, Ohio. Some members of his congregation immediately branded it a throwback to pagan customs. Upset by his resistance to a Christmas decoration traditional in the

churches of his native Hanover, Reverend Schwan decided to have no tree the following year. On Christmas Eve, however, another Cleveland minister, Edwin Canfield, settled the matter in favor of the Christmas tree by having two children deliver a tree to Pastor Schwan and his congregation.

Most early trees were not elaborately and expensively decorated. Many were decorated entirely with simple things like cookies, candy, pinecones, dried seed pods, and strings of popcorn and cranberries. A small yellow apple with shiny red cheeks called a "ladies apple" was a popular tree decoration, and some Penn-

"The Christmas Tree," from an 1864 painting by E. Osborn.

sylvania Dutch farmers' trees were decorated only with homemade doughnuts and strings of dried apple slices. Throughout the nineteenth century German-Americans had a great fondness for paper flowers, paper mottoes, and white sugar animals, often as brightly and imaginatively painted as pieces of Mexican folk art.

The arrival in America of German-made glass balls brought about a major change in the way the American tree was decorated, by introducing the universal Christmas ornament of the twentieth century and triggering the revolutionary shift from homemade to store-bought decorations.

Only one American family in five had a Christmas tree in 1900, although most children probably enjoyed one at their school or at a neighbor's house and undoubtedly wished for one of their own. In the first years of the twentieth century the custom spread like wildfire, and by 1910 in many parts of America, nearly all children had a tree at home. Nevertheless, there were many little towns in the South and in the West where the first tree did not appear until after 1915, and in some areas it was customary to have a church or community-hall tree but rare to see one in the home. There are a surprising number of Americans alive today who never saw a Christmas tree as children and never had their own until they became adults.

By 1930 the tree had become a nearly universal part of the American Christmas. Throughout the Depression, a generation of Americans dug deep into their pockets to give their families a tree like the ones they had loved or desperately wanted as children. Today the big tree in the living room, the little one on the office desk, and the artificial tree without which it wouldn't be Christmas at the roadside hamburger palace all bespeak a deep national love of America's adopted Christmas custom.

From THE CHRISTMAS TREE BOOK by Phillip V. Snyder, Copyright © Phillip Snyder, 1976. Reprinted by permission of The Viking Press.

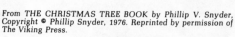

American Christmas Pageantry

Christmas at the White House

Photos, courtesy the White House

Christmas is a time of great joy, a time for family and friends and a time for thought and prayer. Along with the millions of other American families that celebrate this special holiday, the Nation's First Families have traditionally joined in the gaiety with White House festivities conveying to all, the gener-

Christmas Tree in the Blue Room.
Nixon Administration—Christmas 1972.

Christmas Creche in the East Room.
Nixon Administration—Christmas 1972.

osity and goodwill of those who dwell within. Although much political history has been made behind its great doors, we are reminded at this season that the White House has also been a home since 1800 with each new family sharing and celebrating many of their own Yuletide observances and customs with the American people. Sparkling with colorful decorations, spiced with smells of deliciously prepared foods and ringing with the happy sounds of laughter and song, the White House has, since its earliest days, symbolized our country's festive celebration of Christmas.

Nothing typifies the Yuletide spirit more than shining decorations cheerfully adorning our homes. The White House is certainly no exception, and each year the glitter of bright colors and twinkling lights among the evergreens and mistletoe set the atmosphere for

Christmas celebrations.

The first Christmas tree ever to be decorated in the White House was enjoyed by the Benjamin Harrisons in the Oval Room on the second floor of the mansion. Everyone, including the family, staff members and the President himself, decorated the tree with elaborate trimmings of candles and silvery ornaments. The young people frolicked amidst the decorations singing German carols, and the President added to the fun by dressing up as Santa Claus and distributing gifts and goodies.

Gingerbread House in State Dining Room.
Ford Administration—Christmas 1975.

The State Dining Room.
Nixon Administration—Christmas 1972.

Harrison continued to decorate the Presidential residence at Christmastime for the remainder of his term in office, despite the tragic death of his wife in the fall of 1892. His last Christmas in the White House was further dampened when his young granddaughter developed scarlet fever and was quarantined upstairs throughout the season. Nevertheless, with undaunted spirits, he cheered the rest of his family by leading the annual tree decorating ritual.

Since that time, Presidential families have enjoyed the charm and pleasure of a decorated tree, each adding their own special touch and personality to this delightful tradition.

It was the Eisenhowers who set the record for the greatest number of trees in one season—twenty-six! In 1959, Mamie, with her natural enthusiasm, decorated these trees, some with the ornaments and gifts sent to the Eisenhowers by the Communist leader Nikita Khruschev.

State Floor Corridor looking towards the Creche in the East Room.
Nixon Administration—Christmas 1972.

The decorations even extended to the laundry room and the maids' sitting chamber! Their little grandson David had his very own private tree on the third floor to avoid the panic he caused a previous year when he awoke at 3 A.M., squealing with delight over the presents under the tree.

In recent years the First Ladies have selected special themes for the White House Christmas tree. Mrs. Jacqueline Kennedy in 1962 styled a tree after the famous one in Tschaikowsky's "Nutcracker Suite" ballet, hanging sugarplum fairies, toy soldiers and drums as well as cookies and other goodies from every branch. White lights were used to set off the fine ornaments which were made by blind and elderly craftsmen. Tinsel was not used that year for fear that it would hide the colorful details which so greatly thrilled the Kennedy children, Caroline and John-John.

Lady Bird Johnson presented a new

Close-up of tree in the Blue Room.
Nixon Administration—Christmas 1972.

theme with her creation of the Early American Tree. Gingerbread cookies, snowmen, teddy bears, nuts, popcorn, cranberry chains, straw stars, toy soldiers, drums and dried seed pods were among the many ornaments which delighted visitors who passed through the Blue Room in 1966. The gingerbread was real as high as anyone could reach, but on the upper branches, it was ceramic. The following year shiny silver stars, tiny mirrors and balls were added, and little elves were placed under the tree to greet everyone who happened by.

To glorify the spiritual message of the birth of the Christ Child, a beautiful eighteenth-century Italian creche is now displayed in the East Room. This exquisite Nativity scene is composed of thirty hand-carved, baroque, elegantly attired figures, including the Holy Family, the Wise Men, their attendants, the shepherds and angels and all the animals associated with the manger. Donated to the White House during the Johnson Administration, this fine and deeply inspiring work of art has become another meaningful addition to White House Christmases.

The Christmas trees during the Nixon years were a tribute to the fifty American states. The "American Flower Tree" was adorned with velvet and satin ornaments, each bearing a miniature replica of every state's official flower, gem or mineral. In 1970 the theme of the tree was expanded to reflect a special historical note. Gold and lace reproductions of Mrs. Monroe's fans, created by handicapped artisans, were added to the tree which was then moved to the Monroe Room, better known as the Blue Room. These golden ornaments were a beautiful complement to the original gilded Monroe chairs which are located in this chamber.

Another historical addition to the Nixon Christmas decor is the display of the Fanny Hayes Doll House, constructed for President Hayes's young daughter by White House carpenters in 1877.

Not all Presidents have been such en-

Close-up of tree in the Blue Room.
Ford Administration—Christmas 1975.

Christmas Tree in the Blue Room.
Ford Administration—Christmas 1975.

thusiasts for the Christmas tree. Teddy Roosevelt, an ardent conservationist, believed that the practice of cutting trees to decorate homes at Christmas was a wasteful depletion of our forests, and he banned this tradition from the executive mansion in an effort to influence his fellow Americans. Much to his surprise and initial dismay, his young son Archie decided that Christmas was not Christmas without a tree; and the lad smuggled one into the house, decorated it in secrecy and waited until Christmas morning to unveil it. The President, after a few encouraging words from noted conservationist, Gifford Pinchot, admitted that it did lend a festive touch. He then deemed a tree permissible only if it had been cut from an already too dense forest.

The exterior of the White House is also adorned with great splendor and exuberance. Passersby on Pennsylvania Avenue have enjoyed the evergreen-covered lanterns and twinkling lights which set off the north portico. Millions of tourists to the nation's capital, as well as area residents, have happily taken the public tour of the White House to view first-hand the dazzle and luster of their President's home decorated for Christmas. However, it was Mrs. Nixon with her characteristic warmth and friendliness who first arranged special candlelight tours. She opened the doors to thousands for evening visits to the state rooms and enhanced this time with the peaceful strains of live Christmas and classical music.

Bethlehem Steel Corporation

A Star Over Bethlehem, Pennsylvania

'Twas the night before Christmas—nearly 225 years ago—that a little group of Moravian missionaries, gathered in a rude log cabin in the Pennsylvania wilderness, christened their New World home for the birthplace of the Prince of Peace . . . Bethlehem.

The first settlers of Bethlehem, followers of one of the oldest Protestant churches in history, came from Herrnhut,

Germany, with the altruism of true missionaries to the Indians. They had faced hardships and perils to reach this distant land which offered freedom from the religious strife of the Old World. Now, on December 24, 1741, the small band was assembled in its first dwelling, a log cabin, to observe the Vigils of Christmas Eve. In the group was its patron-leader, Count von Zinzendorf, who had come on a visit to Pennsylvania in the hope of uniting the various religious elements there.

During the evening devotions, the imaginative Count was deeply impressed with the similarity of their shelter housing both man and beasts to that in which Jesus was born in the City of David. Impulsively, he seized a lighted taper and led the way to the part where the cattle were kept, singing an old German Epiphany hymn, "Not Jerusalem, Lowly Bethlehem!" The words of the chorale which combined Christmas and missionary thoughts expressed the feeling of the hour; thus the occasion suggested to the worshipers a name for their future home, and by general consent, the place was called Bethlehem.

Bethlehem of today is a typical, progressive, small American city. Naturally, in the course of more than two centuries, some of the customs that were in vogue during the early days of the community have disappeared.

Two of the Moravian features still remaining are the building of "putzes" and the making of the Moravian beeswax Christmas candles.

The "putz" was originally constructed in the home; and today many Bethlehem families still follow the custom each Christmas season. There is also a "putz" built for public viewing, such as the Community Christmas Putz in the gymnasium of Moravian Prep School.

The Bethlehem Community Christmas Putz is built annually by members of the Moravian Church. A "putz" is the Moravian version of the Christmas tree and comes from the German *putzen* meaning "to decorate." It is a miniature portrayal of the Nativity in which the scenes are grouped under a single Christmas tree or many trees with moss as a base for the landscaping. In its erection the creator uses treasured figures of wood or paper-mache, tiny fences, snarled stumps, and rocks carefully kept from year to year; sand, earth, little trees, and sometimes even water, so arranged that the Holy Family, represented in a cave or thatched stable, is always the central subject. Modern scenes and electrical displays such as toy railroads are not part of the authentic "putz."

The beeswax candles are used at the traditional Moravian Christmas Eve vigils, which annually attract many non-members because of the unique and inspirational service of music and prayer.

Weeks are spent in preparation for this particular Yuletide celebration. As early as October, the pouring of thousands of pure beeswax candles is begun by modern-day Moravians. The candle-making itself is a hand process using the same methods and type of molds employed by the early settlers. The tiny candles, which are used in Moravian churches and homes throughout the nation, are supposed to symbolize the coming of Light into the world with the birth of the Christ Child. Those used in the local congregation are trimmed by the women sacristans of the church. Paper frills of different colors are placed around the base for decorative purposes and to prevent hot wax from burning those holding the candles. Last year more than three thousand were used in Bethlehem's historic Central Moravian Church for the traditional Christmas Eve Vigil services.

Visitors to Bethlehem will be able to see the huge Star of Bethlehem on the top of South Mountain overlooking the city.

This Christmas Putz in which figurines tell the Christmas Story is exhibited annually during the Yule Season and is viewed by thousands of visitors to Bethlehem each year.

One of the largest and best lighted community Christmas trees in the nation will again be seen on the Hill-to-Hill bridge. As in past years numerous homes and public buildings will feature a candle in every window. This has caused Bethlehem to become known also as "The Christmas Candle City of America."

The Christmas season observance locally is much like that of any other American city. It does not include a "pageant" or "festival" as some people think. Bethlehem's chief claim to Christmas City fame is its historical background with its non-commercial and dignified observance of the Christmas season in the spirit of goodwill.

All of the churches have special services during the Christmas holidays and Central Moravian Church features a "Putz" display, which is a setting of miniature figures depicting the Nativity story.

High point of Christmas for Moravians of Bethlehem, Pennsylvania, is the Christmas Eve Vigil, a service of music.

For this occasion choirs, orchestra, trombonists, sacristans and their helpers have devoted endless hours of preparations. The church decorations are elaborate and center on a more than life-size painting of the Nativity scene, framed by the great arch behind the pulpit. Sacristans' helpers have decorated thousands of locally-molded beeswax candles with gaily colored

The Gemeinhaus, built in 1741, now houses the Moravian Museum.

Bethlehem Steel Corporation

frills which serve not only to please the eye but also to protect the hand from dripping wax.

The trombonists usher in the service with the playing of Christmas chorales. The choir sings a number of anthems, some by classic German composers, others by eighteenth century Moravian musicians. Choir and congregation join in the singing of many traditional hymns, including the choral, "Not Jerusalem, Lowly Bethlehem," from which Bethlehem received its name.

Two parts of the service are awaited with particular eagerness by the children. One is the singing of the hymn, "Morning Star," in which the soloist is always a child whose selection has been kept a secret. The other is the moment during the latter half of the service when the Sacristans appear with their trays of lighted candles. Each person is given one and the Vigil ends with congregation and choir singing by their friendly light.

SACRISTANS are a group of volunteers who assist in the preparation of services, decorate the church for special events, serve coffee and buns at Love Feasts, and generally help to make the services run smoothly.

THE TROMBONISTS are unusual in that they have in their choir soprano, alto, tenor, bass, and double bass trombones.

A LOVE FEAST is a service of fellowship, consisting of anthems, chorales, hymns, during which coffee and buns are served.

A CHORALE is a special type of hymn. The ones used in the Moravian hymnals are mainly German in origin and have very singable harmony, well suited to a congregation which prefers to sing four-part harmony.

The Star of Bethlehem on the top of South Mountain is the largest display of its kind in the world.

From the city, the display appears as a conventional five-pointed star with eight rays emanating outward. From a distance it appears as a shepherd's star with a bright center mass, hovering over the community. It is visible from the Borough of Wind Gap, twenty miles to the north, while to the south, a few hills and the curvature of the earth are the only limits of visibility.

The center mass, or five-pointed star, is twenty feet in diameter. The main vertical ray is eighty-one feet in height and the main horizontal ray is fifty-three feet long. The shorter diagonal rays are in proportion. A total of 280 fifty-watt, special, clear lamps are used, 140 on a side.

The Star is mounted on a steel structure ninety-one feet high and twenty-five feet by five feet wide at the base. The foundations are embedded in concrete eleven feet below the surface. The entire structure is galvanized to prevent rusting, while the exposed surfaces of the Star are porcelain enamel.

A focal point of the Christmas lighting display is the huge tree at the plaza of the Hill-to-Hill Bridge.

The tree, which captures the eye of motorists from any entrance of the bridge, is composed of 110 smaller evergreen trees taken from the watershed at Wild Creek, thirty-five miles north of Bethlehem and the city's source of water supply.

The tree is fifty-one feet in height and twenty-eight feet in diameter at its base. Construction begins at the top. Additional trees are placed around the concrete pylon to create the appearance of a single tree. Individual trees are partly nailed and partly wired together and mounted on a wooden scaffold.

Illumination comes from 3,000 multicolored lamps.

The man-made tree is the creation of Mr. Joseph M. Daday, Chief City Electrician, and his crew. It is considered one of the most beautiful non-commercial projects of any city in the country.

Its appearance receives annual praise from local residents and visitors to Bethlehem during the Christmas season and is always included in photographs of Bethlehem holiday scenes.

Bethlehem community Christmas tree with the Star of Bethlehem in the background.

Many persons send their Christmas greeting mail to Bethlehem, in order to have the Bethlehem postmark on it. The Postmaster of Bethlehem will be glad to give your mail special attention, if you bundle it up and direct it to his personal attention.

Christmas in Colonial Williamsburg

Photos, courtesy The Colonial Williamsburg Foundation

Wreaths and evergreen garlands galore, enhanced by candlelight at night, decorate windows and doorways to re-create a colonial-style Christmas in this eighteenth-century capital of Virginia.

"Publick" buildings and homes on historic Duke of Gloucester Street are decked each holiday season to add a festive backdrop for the sixty-odd Christmas activities scheduled each year.

The impressive Governor's Palace sets the theme for the decorating of the Historic Area. Here at this one-time residence of seven royal governors, Colonial Williamsburg's flower arranger, Libbey Hodges, hangs many pine garlands and wreaths—from windows and balconies, to the wrought-iron entrance gate. Even the cupola high above the roof has its own wreath.

From the Governor's Palace to the Capitol, houses are decked, wreathed and garlanded. Visitors also see plain wreaths or elaborate ones of fresh fruit and cones along the way in the exhibition buildings and outside on houses decorated by local residents.

Special holiday arrangements adorn the interiors of the Governor's Palace, the Raleigh and Wetherburn Taverns, the George Wythe, Peyton Randolph,

and the Brush-Everard and James Geddy Houses. Miss Hodges adorns mantels with box, pin, or soft-red cedar, bayberry, rosemary, ivy and cherry laurel. Apples and holly, artfully arranged around pewter plates, often decorate mantels too. She tops old prints with sprigs of holly tucked in firmly between the picture frame and wall.

At Christmas and throughout the year, Miss Hodges uses only materials known here in Virginia in the eighteenth century. She bases her arrangements on period prints and, in general, follows old English traditions spiced with trimmings mentioned in colonial records. Miss Hodges's holiday arrangements, too, reflect the symmetry in design that colonists brought from England and applied whenever possible to their gardens.

To transform Williamsburg for the holidays, Miss Hodges and her assistants decorate hundreds of plain boxwood or pine wreaths. Often fresh fruit known to the colonists is added to execute Della Robbia wreaths inspired by the fifteenth-century artist. The semi-tropical fruits seen here today—oranges, limes, lemons and pineapples—were available two-hundred years ago from the West Indies. Visitors, however, are surprised to find so many decorations with pomegranates. This fruit was recorded by colonial naturalist, Mark Catesby, as "in great perfection in the Gardnes of the Hon. William Byrd, Esq.; in the freshes of James river."

Exhibition buildings gradually take on "holiday garb" about a week before Christmas when the traditional "Grand Illumination of the City" officially opens the holiday season. Once the New Year arrives, the wreaths and garlands dis-

Colonial carolers on an evening stroll.

appear, candles no longer shine in the windows, and Yuletide visitors return home with memories of a very real old-fashioned Christmas.

The magnificent buildings of Colonial Williamsburg in their winter settings, the historic homes decorated with wreaths of laurel, ivy and holly, as well as the townspeople dressed in colorful costumes, recall Christmas as it existed in America over two hundred years ago. During Williamsburg's holiday celebration which lasts a fortnight, ceremonies and customs, such as the Grand Illumination, are reenacted to capture the enduring charm and beauty of a Colonial Christmas. In *Christmas on the American Frontier*, John E. Baur reveals how this was also a time for merriment and feasting:

Virginia, at its first and finest colonial flowering in Williamsburg, the capital, probably celebrated Christmas in a more magnificent and patrician way than any other American colony. Here, where there was wealth and leisure enough for elegance and the courtly manner which must accompany it, the air of eighteenth-century English aristocracy was imported to tidewater North America.

On Christmas morning one might expect a large and early breakfast, followed by a fox hunt, indulged in by the gentlemen in powdered wigs, gold lace, and scarlet waistcoats. The crisp and bracing air and the exercise produced an appetite fit for the pleasures of the table which awaited.

Christmas dinner was fashionably early at half past three in the afternoon. And it was a wondrous meal! Food was abundant and always varied. Not far from the plantation, wild geese abounded. As each large estate used a river for transportation, fish were always nearby, and up that same stream came vessels laden with spice from the Indies, East and West, and familiar foodstuffs from Old England. In came dish after dish, and finally, the plum pudding and the mince pie arrived. In later years a wild stranger from the New World, roast turkey, graced the long and well-attended table.

Men may change their dress and their tools to fit more appropriately a new land, and adopt fresh jargons to explain their new livelihoods, but last of all do they modify their religion and the ancient ways of keeping its great days. And so it was that the Virginia Christmas, not only in foodstuffs but even in decorations, was Merry England on the Potomac or the James. Here one might see again garlands of English ivy and the holly wreath, which is said to stand for the crown of thorns, its berries for drops of blood.

Ever since the Druids had considered it sacred, the English had honored the mistletoe, and we shall never know how many maidens on both sides of the water were wooed and won under its unobtrusive blossoms.

Once they had rested awhile after the hearty adventures of an overly rich dinner, Englishmen of Britain as well as those of the colonies loved their Christmastime games. Today they seem rather naive pastimes, including as they did such children's diversions as blindman's buff and hunt the slipper, but even sophisticated Virginians sometimes unbent to engage in them. Present giving, however, was not as extensive a custom as it has since become. Usually only sweethearts and children were remembered with special gifts.

Over the years a wide variety of decorations have graced the Center's trees. Tinsel, ornaments and the traditional holiday garlands have been employed as well as plastic globes, foil spangles and plastic stars. Traditionally, except during the blackout days of World War II, the trees have been decorated with thousands of brightly colored lights. The lighting ceremony, usually taking place in the first or second week of December, is a festive affair and attracts thousands of excited spectators.

Christmas trees, however, are not the only spectacular attractions in Rockefeller Center during the Christmas season. Since 1933 music and pageantry have shared the spotlight. With the appearance in 1933 of the Paulist Choristers, Choir of the Church of the Heavenly Rest, the Columbia University Glee Club and the Gloria Trumpeters, a long tradition of community singing around the decorated Center began. In 1939 the Rockefeller Center Choristers, a group of men and women whose business homes are in Rockefeller Center, furnished the Christmas music. This concert became a traditional event and continued for twenty-one years. A multitude of church choirs, glee clubs, opera stars, service choirs, barbershop quartets, folk choirs and popular vocalists have supplemented their efforts in the past and continue the tradition of holiday music to the present.

In 1936 the Rockefeller Plaza outdoor ice skating pond was opened to the public. Since then an annual Rockefeller Center skating pageant has been held. In 1938 "Hans Brinker on the Silver Skates" was presented in pantomime on the skating pond. In addition, many skating exhibitions have been featured. World figure skating champion Carol Heiss appeared in 1959 and stars from the Ice Follies and Holiday on Ice have made several appearances in recent years.

Rockefeller

Christmas 1961.

De Wys, Inc.

Center Celebration

Right: Rockefeller Center's famed aluminum angels sparkle along the Center's channel gardens. Bottom: Skating on the channel's ice rink is a popular pastime during every Christmas celebration at the Center.

Christmas trees at Rockefeller Center have ranged from fifty-foot pines to ninety-foot Norway spruces and have been viewed by approximately 2,500,000 spectators annually. The decorations and lighting effects have covered a wide variety of colors and schemes. In addition to the holiday decorations, Christmas musical programs at Rockefeller Center have been planned over the years to create for New Yorkers a unique community activity reminiscent of traditional hometown caroling in the village square.

The celebraton of Christmas at Rocke-

the shape of the tree. Since that time, New Yorkers have not known a Christmas without a tree and accompanying celebration in Rockefeller Center.

Christmas trees have come from several states and Canada during this time. New Jersey and Vermont have supplied eleven trees, New Hampshire, Maine, Massachusetts, Pennsylvania and Connecticut have supplied eight, and Canada provided a beautiful sixty-four-foot white spruce in 1966 in honor of the centennial of its confederation in 1967. The remainder of the trees have come from New York.

Beginning in 1939, the pools, fountains and gardens of the Center's channel have also become sources of decoration. Twenty six-foot ivory candles were lighted along the pools, and in 1940, replicas of golden organ pipes, six to nine feet high, stood in the channel between the British Empire Building and La Maison Francaise. Multicolored plastic globes were placed upon a carpet of pine and spruce boughs in the six channel garden beds in 1946. In 1954, twelve nine-foot angels, sculptured in aluminum, copper and brass wire, holding aloft five-foot trumpets, decorated the channel gardens. In 1961, round and jolly snowmen, seven to nine feet high, paraded along the channel and returned in 1962 for an encore. Other decorations such as giant, sculptured medieval figures, Santa and his sleigh, and a multitude of archways and ornamental trees have graced the garden.

For the first time in 1951 the lighting ceremonies were viewed on television by millions. Kate Smith pressed the button which turned on the tree lights and flood lighting. From 1953 to 1955 the lighting festivities took place on the nationwide Howdy Doody program. In 1967, the lighting was seen for the first time throughout the United States and Canada.

feller Center started informally in 1931 when a small tree was placed on the site of the British Empire Building and La Maison Francaise soon after demolition of brownstones in that area had been completed. It was decorated with tinsel and gaily colored ornaments, and an early photo shows workmen lined up around the tree to receive their pay on Christmas Eve.

The first formal tree was erected in 1933 on the sidewalk in front of the seventy-story RCA Building (completed that May) and was decorated with 700 blue and white electric lights focused in

Roasting meat at the 1784 Salem Tavern.

𝔄𝔫 𝔒𝔩𝔡 𝔖𝔞𝔩𝔢𝔪 𝔜𝔲𝔩𝔢

Winston-Salem, North Carolina

Photos by Old Salem, Inc.

A typical early nineteenth-century meal at the 1819 John Vogler House.

The sights, sounds and smells of Christmastime long ago are re-created each December in Old Salem, restored Moravian congregation town.

Called "Salem Christmas" the one-day event is a part of the program of interpretation of Old Salem, Inc., the non-profit organization responsible for the restoration and operation of the old Moravian town.

Research has shown that most of the Christmas activities in eighteenth- and early nineteenth-century Salem were centered in the church where special services were held and where today many of these traditional forms of worship still are observed at Christmas. Outside the church, though, Christmas in Salem was largely a continuation of the closely knit community life as it was lived day by day.

The craftsmen worked at their benches. The women cooked and spun. The night watchman made his hourly rounds. The children studied their lessons. Frequently, music could be heard coming from trombone choirs on the streets or from singers and instrumentalists inside the homes. And over all, the spirit of peace and brotherly love was clearly evident.

It is this simple, unhurried, warm-hearted atmosphere that "Salem Christmas" seeks to recapture by re-creating the character of the town as it was nearly 200 years ago.

The streets of the historic area are blocked to traffic so that visitors may walk in the streets as well as along the brick sidewalks. Occasionally, a covered wagon rumbles past, offering rides to

Old Salem Moravian Band.

children; or a horse clops by, its rider wearing early Moravian dress and often carrying a lantern. A night watchman strolls the streets, blowing a conch shell and calling the hours with chants written in the eighteenth century in Saxony and brought to America by the Moravians. Bands move from corner to corner, playing traditional Christmas chorals and carols. Visiting children are invited to roll hoops, fly kites and play other old games on Salem Square. In an open area, a pig roasts on a spit and, nearby, a craftsman demonstrates how candles were dipped. Lighting for the event is by torches, lanterns and candles.

Five of the restored buildings in Old Salem are open, with special activities

In typical eighteenth-century garb, participants in Old Salem's Christmas festivities roast a pig.

Fiddle playing in the 1771 Miksch Tobacco Shop.

typical of early Salem going on in each— baking, coffee roasting, needlework, and craftsmen working at tinsmithing, joinery, gunsmithing, pottery. A special feature is the music, by chorus, organ, vocal soloists, flutes, recorders, harpsi-chord, string quartet, and guitar.

All participants are in early Moravian dress, but spectators also become a part of the event as they join in the singing and stop to chat with friends—just as did the people in the early years of Salem.

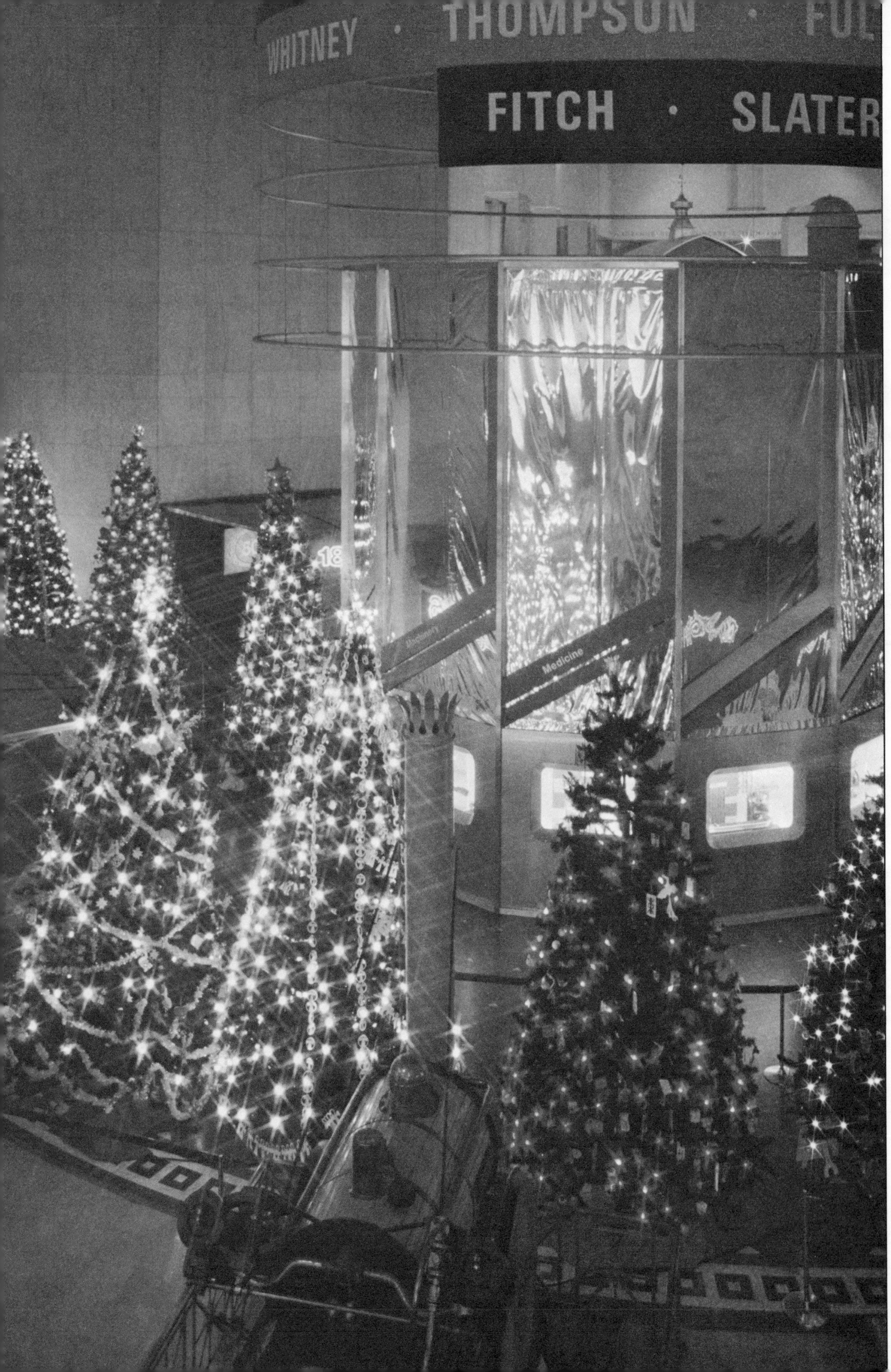
WHITNEY · THOMPSON
FITCH · SLATER
Medicine

Opposite: *Decorated trees ring the Museum's rotunda.*
Top: *A Latvian tree decorated by a traditionally garbed Latvian miss.* Right: *A Polish Creche.*

Christmas Around the World: Chicago Style

Photos by Michael Philip Manheim

For three and a half decades, during the Christmas season, visitors to the Museum of Science and Industry have been delighted by the sights and sounds of the "Christmas Around the World" festival.

The Festival was initiated in 1942 by the late Maj. Lenox Lohr, then the Museum's president, to add a bright note for Chicago's citizens during the war years and to recognize the city's many ethnic groups.

Another exhibit that shows a Christmas touch, the gigantic model train layout has its own miniature Christmas tree that complements the full-scale trees on display in the rotunda beyond.

The festival was not always known by the name it carries today. Old flyers show that visitors in 1943 came to see "Christmas in the United Nations." In 1944 the event was called "Around the World at Christmas."

The very first festival, which began December 11, 1942, featured one tree that was redecorated daily to represent another country. Holiday meals, a favorite feature today, were served during the lunch hours. Foods from the day's featured nation were offered in the Museum's cafeteria.

Flags from twenty-nine countries were hung from the North Court balcony, adding another colorful note to that first festival.

Among the nations represented in that first year were Greece, Mexico, Czechoslovakia, Yugoslavia, Russia, the Netherlands, Belgium, Poland, the British Empire, China, various South American nations, and the United States.

Theater pageants were added to the festival in its second year, and the ethnic dinners were moved to the evening hours. In that year, many trees circled the Rotunda, one for each of the lands represented.

The first five festivals were each held for two-week periods, beginning in mid-December and continuing until close to Christmas. The decision was made in

1946 to expand the event and begin it earlier, on the day after Thanksgiving. This has remained the traditional opening day ever since.

During the late 1940s and 1950s, cooking demonstrations were presented during "Christmas Around the World." Members of the participating ethnic groups showed visitors how to prepare various foods from their countries. These afternoon programs were given by the country whose menu was highlighted by that day's holiday dinner.

As the years have passed, the festival has grown until today there are thirty-four ethnic groups and nationalities participating, a record number. Attendance during the holiday period has skyrocketed, from 130,000 in December of 1942 to well over 585,000 in 1975.

With its growth and changes, the festival's basic format and purpose remain the same. It still sparkles with the joy that is Christmas, and it still speaks of hope for understanding among all the nations of the world.

During the Festival, many Museum displays show Christmas touches. A miniature Christmas tree stands within the gates of Colleen Moore Hargrave's famous "Fairy Castle." The well-known silent screen actress had the castle started in 1928 as a home for her extensive collection of miniatures. Seven years—and over half a million dollars later, the nine square foot palace was completed, down to running water in the bathrooms and kitchen. The castle was donated by Mrs. Hargrave to the Museum as a Christmas gift to the children of the world.

The Blessing of the Waters

Photos by O. Y. Thomas, Tarpon Springs Leader

Tradition is a treasured way of life in Tarpon Springs, home port of Florida's picturesque sponge fleet on the Sun Coast.

And the celebration of Epiphany each January 6 is a memorable and colorful tradition which enriches the lives of the city's Greek-American residents and, at the same time, provides a beautiful, deeply moving ceremony for the thousands of spectators who come to view the annual rites.

Rich in pageantry and steeped in religious significance, the ceremonial commemorates the baptism of Jesus by John the Baptist in the river Jordan. It all began in the Old World, where the silver cross was thrown into the waters of the Aegean Sea to symbolize this important event, while doves flew heavenward to represent the flight of Christ's spirit to His Father.

As hundreds of Greek immigrants settled in Tarpon Springs at the turn of the century, they brought with them this honored observance.

At Spring Bayou, whose sloping banks form a natural amphitheater, the exciting and highly competitive Diving for the Cross ceremony is reenacted. It is the highlight of the Epiphany Day celebration, known also as Greek Cross Day.

Following a brief religious ceremony on the pier, the archbishop casts a gilded

Parade preceding the day's festivities.

Top left: The archbishop leads a brief religious ceremony on the banks of Spring Bayou in preparation for the tossing of the cross into the Bayou waters. Top right: As the cross hits the water, the divers, who have been waiting in boats and in the water, dive to secure it. Bottom left: Cross in hand, the wet but happy diver climbs ashore to receive his blessing from the archbishop. Bottom right: The diver's blessing.

wooden cross into the waters. A white dove is released simultaneously. Young divers of the Greek community, who have signed up weeks in advance for the opportunity, vie for the honor of recovery.

Clad in swim trunks and white shirts emblazoned with the words "Epiphany Day," the intent young men wait on board gaily painted boats or in the water. As members of the clergy chant an appropriate hymn and the bishop throws the cross, the divers hit the water.

The weighted cross is usually retrieved within a matter of seconds, amid a great flurry of thrashing and scrambling. It is believed that good fortune will remain with the successful diver and his family throughout the ensuing year. The struggle of the young men is, according to tradition, symbolic of man's effort to find salvation. The triumphant diver receives a special blessing at the pier, and again during the concluding religious ceremonies at the church.

This reenactment is only a part of the

The dove has long been used in Epiphany celebrations in the Greek Orthodox Church to symbolize the ascent of Christ's spirit to the Father in heaven. Young girls carry these doves in the parades marking the opening of Epiphany festivities.

day's events, however. Religious services in St. Nicholas Greek Orthodox Church begin early in the morning. Magnificently robed clergymen officiate, and the all-girl Byzantine choir sings the ancient hymns of the faith. For the benefit of the many visitors, the eleven o'clock sermon is delivered in English. A loudspeaker relays the message outside, as the church cannot accommodate the large number of people who gather for the religious rites.

Shortly after noon, the Blessing of the Waters ceremony is held in the front of the white marble kiosk in the church courtyard. It is identical to the traditional Epiphany rite performed in the Greek church since the first days of Christianity.

A colorful parade then forms and proceeds to Spring Bayou. Included in the procession are church dignitaries, led by the Bishop. His robes are decorated with bells, similar to the robes of the high priest Aaron. In his hand he carries the serpent-twined crosier symbolizing the the serpent lifted by Moses in the wilderness.

Elsewhere in the procession are the acolytes, representatives of various foreign countries and Greek organizations, groups of children dressed in the national costumes of Greece, the Byzantine choir, the official dove carrier and special guests.

The short benedictory service at the church, following the recovery of the cross, concludes the religious services. The remainder of the day belongs to the Greek people themselves. A *glendi* (Greek festival) is held in the sponge market at the sponge docks. Greek food is served and *bouzoukia* music and Greek dancing continue until dark.

The annual Epiphany Ball held that night signifies the end of Epiphany or Greek Cross Day—an ancient, beautiful ceremonial as rich in tradition as the people themselves.

Cross divers assemble in front of St. Nicholas Greek Orthodox Church.

Christmas at the Tabernacle

Photos, courtesy LDS Church

During the Christmas season, Temple Square in Salt Lake City blooms with more than a hundred thousand delicate pastel lights in shrubs, trees, and along the walkways surrounding the world-famous Temple (on the right) and domed Tabernacle (on the left). The breathtaking Christmas lighting display has been a fixture on Temple Square since 1965.

During the spring, summer and autumn, Salt Lake City's ten-acre Temple Square is a peaceful, lushly landscaped, walled-in haven providing an escape from worldly pressures for the local folks as well as the three million out-of-towners who visit every year.

At Christmastime, when the bloom is gone from the lawns, gardens, trees and shrubs, the Square blooms anew; but this time the beauty is provided by more than a hundred thousand delicate pastel lights. The lights twinkle from the shrubs, the trees, and along the winding walks that carry you through the historic mecca of the Mormons.

The breathtaking Christmas lighting display has been a fixture on Temple Square since 1965, and many people from around the country plan special visits to the Utah capital in the winter, rather than the tourist season, just to see the lights.

The switching on of the lights for the Christmas season is coupled with the traditional Christmas Youth Songfest as the inaugural event in a series of holiday activities on the square. The Songfest

The 375-member Mormon Tabernacle Choir. In the background is the famous

features nearly 5,000 young singers from high school choruses in Salt Lake City and other communities along the western slope of the Rocky Mountains, singing a variety of Christmas music, accompanied by a full symphony orchestra and the famous 10,000-pipe Tabernacle organ. The event is sponsored by the Mormons—The Church of Jesus Christ of Latter-day Saints—but open to young singers of all faiths. It is essentially a community event. It is made unique by the fact that the singers virtually fill the cavernous, dome-shaped Mormon Tabernacle. Since there are few seats left for an audience, the Songfest is televised locally, both live and on a delayed basis, so the singers, their families and the general public can enjoy the performance.

Another highlight of the season on Temple Square is the annual Christmas concert by the world famous Mormon Tabernacle Choir. The 375 singers blend their voices in Yuletide song in a show that is free to the public.

10,000 pipe Tabernacle Organ. Inset: The Mormon Youth Symphony and Chorus.

The youthful counterpart of the Tabernacle Choir, the Mormon Youth Symphony and Chorus, caps a busy year of recordings and television shows with another free Christmas concert. The 100-member orchestra and 300 singers—all under thirty years of age—offer more of a middle-of-the-road program than the older, more established Tabernacle Choir, yet maintain the dignity of the occasion.

The Church's children's organization has presented family Christmas theatrical shows in the Tabernacle from time to time. Other local theater groups have also participated in the Temple Square Christmas tradition, presenting classics such as *Amahl and the Night Visitors*, and other shows.

Perhaps the climactic event of the Christmas season on Temple Square is the traditional rendering of Handel's *Messiah* by the Oratorio Society of Utah.

All programs on Temple Square during the Christmas season are free to the public, except for the *Messiah* for which a nominal fee is charged to pay the expense of the Oratorio Society.

A plaza in Santa Fe alight with hundreds of luminarias. In the background is the ancient Palace of the Governors, built in 1610.

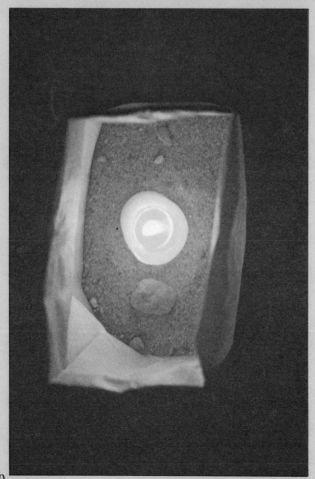

New Mexico's Luminarias

Photos by James Leonard

In the northern part of the state—in Santa Fe, Española, Taos, and the small mountain villages—they call them *farolitos* (little lanterns). And the tall, kindling-wood edifices that are torched into bonfires—those are know as *luminarias* (festival lights or illuminations).

But elsewhere, New Mexico's little paper bag and candle lanterns are universally known as *luminarias*. (And blithely miscalled *luminarios, luminar-*

A candle, a sack, some sand—a luminaria.

A typically decorated Albuquerque adobe: Christmas lights and luminarias.

ros, luminaries and a multitude of other things!)

Both names have respectable backgrounds, and *luminarias*—which, despite some scholarly nitpicking, can be stretched to mean our festive paper bags —looks like the winner, if only because of the numbers of people using the term.

It is sunset on Christmas Eve. At the Village of Tularosa, the asphalt ribbons of US 54 from the north and US 70 from the east marry and travel south towards Alamogordo.

A Christmas Tree in Santa Fe surrounded by luminarias.

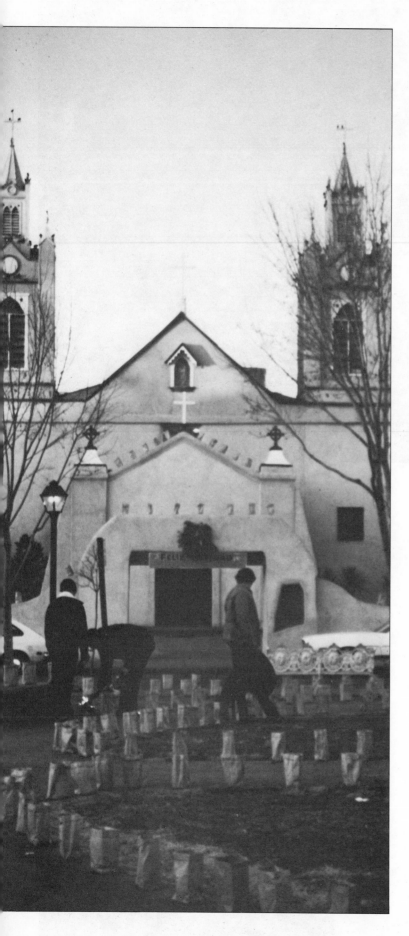

At each end of the village are flashing red lights, and one almost expects to see them joined by green lights, in keeping with the season, as various police agencies man temporary roadblocks.

All street and business lights are off. Only yellow parking lights are allowed as traffic moves slowly through the darkened village.

Once again, it's *luminaria* time.

The glow of thousands of candles lights the village. On walls and rooflines, along paths and drives, around churches, businesses and homes, the soft candlelight shines.

Nearly 12,500 *luminarias* lined the highways through Tularosa in 1973, and more than 30,000 were displayed around the village. More than 50,000 will be lit this Christmas Eve.

Far to the north, in Española, the same Christmas Eve celebration is taking place, as it is in large sections of Albuquerque, where whole neighborhoods become candlelit wonderlands.

They're simple to make, New Mexico's lanterns. Just a few dozen—or hundred! —paper sandwich bags, some sand or dirt, and votive candles. But they're probably more expensive and time-consuming in the long run than it would be to hang out and plug in strings of blinking neon Japanese lights each year.

They take a lot of work.

And they last only a few hours.

Are they worth it?

Just ask the millions of people who go out in the chill dark night to see again the magic lights of Christmas Eve.

The message of Christmas shines clear in New Mexico's little lanterns.

"They're lighting the way for the Christ Child," say the old people as the young ones fill the bags and light the candles.

From NEW MEXICO MAGAZINE, November/December 1974. Reprinted with permission.

Volunteers place and light the luminarias around Albuquerque's Old Town Plaza.

Drive along nearly any street in nearly any town in New Mexico on Christmas Eve, and you'll see houses lined with *luminarias*. These simple decorations consist only of a lighted candle set on a small pile of sand inside an ordinary paper bag, but the effect is lovely. The tradition they represent dates back to the first Christmases celebrated on this continent by the Spanish missionaries of the sixteenth century.

On those early Christmas Eves, the mission priests directed the lighting of little bonfires along the path to the church, "to light the way for the Christ Child." The bonfires were called *luminarias*: Spanish for "lights."

American merchants in the 1800s introduced tallow candles, used in place of the bonfires, and called *farolitos*. Many people feel this term is more "correct" than *luminarias* in describing the modern custom.

Finally, this century contributed the lowly paper sack, the kind used in many supermarket vegetable sections. With a lighted candle inside, they give off an enchanting, dancing yellow glow.

The bags are placed at regular intervals around the roof (the flat adobe buildings lend themselves well to this practice), and along the sidewalk. Sometimes designs are made, usually in the shape of the cross. A little sand is poured in to weight each bag, then a small, wide candle is placed on the sand. At dusk, the candles are lit and the show begins (as well as a vigil of unending maintenance). Tradition requires that they be lit on Christmas Eve, but many people begin a week earlier and continue through New Year's.

James Leonard

Christmas Day in Santa Fe Plaza brings the sight of scores of luminarias set and ready to light.

SAN FRANCISCO'S GREAT DICKENS FAIR

Photos, courtesy the Art Blum Agency

A Dickensian world of winding London streets with quaint and festooned shops, bubbling entertainments from the high to the low, and costumed throngs in top hats and elegant dresses are all part of the heartwarming Victorian holiday enchantment unfolding soon at the Great Dickens Christmas Fair & Pickwick Comic Annual.

This annual re-creation of Christmas Past runs for six fun-filled weekends, remaining snug inside Ol' Fezziwig's immense warehouse at the San Francisco Produce Market.

Top: *Performers in the Victoria and Albert Bijou Music Hall production. Left: Samuel Pickwick emphatically makes a point in one of his many discourses on holiday delights. Bottom: Dr. Brittanicus's renowned Patent Medicine Show.*

Dozens of "amazements to amuse and delight" fill the Fair's five stages with invigorating Yuletide cheer.

Brightening an existence too often grim and dreary, The Penny Gaff Theatre offers continuous bills of variety entertainment. Grand old songs like "She Was Poor but She Was Honest" and "When Father Papered the Parlour" are interpreted by the finest of music hall artists and visitors are invited to sing along.

And, there's more in the Penny Gaff—acrobats and dancers, comic recitations, brass bands and Dr. Brittanicus's Renowned (and new) Patent Medicine Show.

The elegant Victoria and Albert Bijou Music Hall offers several unique productions, including the traditional British holiday extravaganza of scenic spectacle magical transformation—the Christmas pantomime, or Harlequinade.

All the family, down to the youngest of wide-eyed toddlers will enjoy the tale of fair Columbine captured in the Unfrequented Wood by the wicked Spider King; Harlequin's and Puss 'n' Boots's quest for the Pearl of Great Price guarded by the Demons of the Deep; their epic battle with pirates (yes, pirates!) and the final confrontation in the sumptuous Oriental Castle on the Mysterious Isle of Jewels.

This "Celebrated Theatre of Variety" also offers an array of Songs of the Heart and Ballads of Tender Meaning, stirring

A Victorian gentleman's leisure was often taken up playing a game of chance as is this modern day Victorian gentleman at the Great Dickens Christmas Fair.

The secrets of Father Christmas shall only be revealed to this pretty girl at the Great Dickens Christmas Fair.

Irish music, and on Saturday nights (adults only, please) Bawdy Songs of the London Pub and the Saucy French Postcard Tableaux Review or "The Secret Life of Horatio Puddingforth, Esq."

From Fezziwig's Dance Party Hall can be heard the sounds of pleasure as fairgoers join in quadrilles, polkas, jigs and reels and parlor games; and from Mad Sal's Ale House, where the low life hang out and the highborn drop in, a ragged cheer comes up from the rollickers as a small band takes its place on the barrel-framed stage, assuring one and all that London's Irish population is well represented.

The Sisters Worthington, who founded "The Society for the Elevation and Edification of the Working Man," provide a rich fare of stirring recitations, highly edifying lectures, lessons in elocutionary gesticulation and, of course, readings including appearances by Charles Dickens and that worthy gentleman

Fresh fish and chips are a favorite at the Dickens Christmas Fair.

Samuel Pickwick, Esq. to discourse on holiday delights.

An endless parade of Yuletide sights and sounds, together with a tempting array of traditional holiday foods, bracing beverages, and an old English marketplace, form the backdrop for a veritable feast of popular entertainments from the period immortalized for all time by the mighty pen of Charles Dickens.

It's a joyous bustling world, inhabited by the likes of Charles Dickens himself, the young Disraeli, Scrooge, Tiny Tim, Charles Darwin, Queen Victoria (with the entire Royal Family), and literally hundreds more Victorian Londoners in full costume. Parades and processions continually weave through the holiday revelers—Father Christmas with his many attendants, the traditional Boar's Head procession and Mother Goose with her many new characters.

Such is the merriest of Yuletide frolic in this re-creation of Christmas Past at the Great Dickens Christmas Fair & Pickwick Comic Annual.

Main Street, U.S.A.
- A Disney Christmas

Photos by Michael Philip Manheim

An old-fashioned Christmas season filled with excitement, themed parades, extended operating hours and fireworks highlight Walt Disney World's Yuletide activities.

Featured are the famous Disney characters, Toy Soldiers from Babes in Toyland and Santa himself, riding high in a toy-filled sleigh pulled by eight silly reindeer.

Christmas garlands, Della Robbia wreaths and a sixty-five-foot tree festooned with candy canes and gingerbread men adorn Main Street, U.S.A.

MERRY CHRISTMAS

Grateful acknowledgment is here made of the following chambers of commerces and tourist bureaus without whose generosity and assistance this book would not have been possible: The Altadena Chamber of Commerce, Greater Bethlehem Area Chamber of Commerce, Missouri Division of Tourism, Seattle Chamber of Commerce, Greater Tarpon Springs Chamber of Commerce, Department of Development Services—State of Utah, Greater Wilmington Chamber of Commerce and the Winston-Salem Chamber of Commerce. The editors of this volume are particularly indebted to the following foundations, museums, associations, benevolent societies and religious organizations for their invaluable assistance: The Art Blum Agency—Debbie Kendrick, the Chicago Museum of Science and Industry, Christmas Tree Lane Association, Inc.—Charles L. Haynes, The Colonial Williamsburg Foundation, Office of Public Communication—Church of the Latter Day Saints, Macy's Department Store, Old Salem, Inc., Rockefeller Center, Inc., St. Nicholas Greek Orthodox Church—Rev. Tryfon Theophilopoulos and the White House. We also wish to thank the following photo agencies and photographers whose cooperation and generosity are deeply appreciated: Ed Carlin, Patrick Grace, Grant Heilman, Inc., Harold M. Lambert Studios, James S. Leonard and Carol Manheim.

Cover illustration by Lorraine Wells. All photographs, not otherwise credited, by Ideals Publishing Corp.